CONTENTS

Introduction

In a world with a "get thin quick" mentality, it can be easy to fall into dieting traps. Protein bars, protein shakes, low-fat cereals, low-sugar cookies... They become "quick fixes" on our dieting journeys. But ultimately, these "diet foods" are void of nutrients and contribute to our weight gain epidemic, our sugar addictions, and—unfortunately—to our loss of funds. Those protein bars aren't exactly cheap. And they're doing more harm to your body than good.

The 30 day whole food challenge eliminates all processed, sugary foods from your diet, asking you to eat only meat, vegetables, fruits, nuts, and oils. These foods have been proven to restore gut health, add vibrant nutrients and vitamins to your diet, reduce the effects of aging on your skin and organs, and—of course—help with weight loss. That means that some of the diet "staples" still regarded as healthy—such as peanut butter and hummus—are out.

It's been proven that if you just take a "pause" on your normal diet plan for 30 days, you can instill new habits. You won't reach for preservative-rich foods, because your body will crave vegetables, good fats, and proteins. You'll actually train your brain to want healthy foods, rather than quick-fixes at the store.

Fortunately, with the air fryer, you can make some of your favorite "fatty" dishes, all without the calories. You can make sweet potato fries, avocado fries, and kale chips—for a bit of "snacking," and you can treat yourself to yummy Indian dishes, meatballs, a new version of "pizza," spicy pork chops, and, of course, a whole host of vegetable side dishes. And you can do it in record time, with the air fryer: an appliance that circulates hot air throughout the compartment during the cooking cycle.

But the air fryer doesn't just "fry." It also bakes, can cook anything in a soufflé pan or baking dish (as long as the dish fits inside, of course)—like lasagna and meatloaf, and can grill anything, such as a shish kebab or burgers.

Of course, as with anything, the air fryer has a few limitations. It's essential to make sure that, when coating things like sweet potato fries in a kind of "batter" (here, we often use almond flour—a whole food alternative to other breading), to shake off any excess bits, so that they don't smoke. Also, you should always dry off your meats and fishes prior to cooking.

With 30 days of the whole food program, you can expect to have more energy, a decrease in migraines and headaches, fewer gastrointestinal problems, better blood pressure, better cholesterol levels, and, of course, a decreased waistline. It's essential that you don't step on the scale throughout this diet challenge. It's better to fix your thoughts about food—making lifestyle changes, rather than focusing on the number on the scale. It's only a reading of your gravitational pull, anyway. It's better to work from the inside, out, upping your nutritional game, and letting the pounds fall away from there.

Good luck on your diet journey. You deserve the most nutritional, vibrant foods. And this book can help.

.

Whole Food Air Fryer Breakfast Recipes

Eggs in Avocado Boats

Recipe Makes 2 Servings.
Preparation Time: 10 minutes

Ingredients:

2 avocados, medium-sized

4 eggs, small

1 tsp. dried parsley

1 tsp. salt

1 tsp. pepper

Directions:

First slice each avocado in half, removing the center pit. Season the insides with salt, pepper, and parsley.

Next, crack each egg into the center portion of the avocado. Then place each avocado into the air fryer.

Cook the avocado boats in the air fryer for eight minutes at 325 degrees Fahrenheit.

Remove the avocado boats from the air fryer and serve warm with additional salt and pepper.

Whole Food "Egg Bake"

Recipe Makes 8 Servings.
Preparation Time: 30 minutes

Ingredients:

1 pound turkey sausage

1/2 diced onion

2 tsp. coconut oil

1 diced green pepper

3 cups radish hash browns (see other recipe)

1 diced red pepper

10 eggs

1/2 cup almond milk

1 tsp. salt

1 tsp. pepper

Directions:

First, preheat the air fryer to 350 degrees Fahrenheit.

First, add the turkey sausage to a skillet and heat on medium-high. Cook, stirring occasionally, until it's browned. Next, remove it from the skillet and place it on a plate, over the top of a paper towel. Allow it to drain on the paper towel.

Next, add the coconut oil to the skillet. Allow it to melt on medium-high heat, and then cook the peppers and onion for five minutes.

In a medium-sized bowl, whisk together the almond milk, egg, salt, and pepper. Stir in the ground sausage, discarding the greasy paper towel.

Add the pepper mixture into a pan. Top them with the egg mixture.

Place the pan in the air fryer. Cook the egg bake for 20 minutes in the air fryer. When the timer sounds, check that the inside of the egg bake is cooked all the way through. If not, place back in the air fryer for 3 to 5 minutes, or until it's firm.

Serve the egg bake warm, and enjoy.

No-Potato Hashbrowns

Recipe Makes 6 Servings.
Preparation Time: 15 minutes

Ingredients:

1 1/2 pound radishes

2 onions

1 tsp. onion powder

1 tsp. garlic powder

1/2 tsp. salt

1 tsp. paprika

1 tbsp. olive oil

Directions:

First, slice off the radishes at the root, and slice the radishes in a food processor. Proceed with the onions, processing them well in the food processor.

Next, stir the olive oil with the radishes and the onion, making sure to coat the vegetables. Add the radishes and the onion to the bottom of the air fryer at this time.

Next, cook the vegetables in the air fryer at 350 degrees Fahrenheit for ten minutes. Shake the air fryer every two minutes to make sure that the vegetables are cooked on all sides.

Pour the radishes and onion into a mixing bowl, and add the onion powder, the garlic powder, salt, and paprika. Stir well.

Serve the "hashbrowns" warm, and enjoy.

Cinnamon and Coconut Bananas

Recipe Makes 4 Servings.
Preparation Time: 12 minutes

Ingredients:

4 bananas, ripe

1 tsp. cinnamon

1/2 cup almond flour

1 cup coconut flakes, shredded

2 eggs

1 tbsp. coconut oil, melted

Directions:

First, slice each of the bananas into thirds. Pour the almond flour into a small plate or bowl.

Crack the eggs into a side bowl, and whisk them, breaking the yolk. Next, stir together the cinnamon and the coconut in another bowl or plate.

Next, dip each of the bananas into the almond flour. Shake them, and then dip them into the eggs. Make sure the bananas are well-coated.

Then, roll the banana in the cinnamon and coconut mixture, fully coating them as well.

Melt the coconut oil, and drizzle the coconut oil over the bananas. Add the bananas to the air fryer basket at this time.

Air fry the bananas for 12 minutes at 275 degrees Fahrenheit. Afterwards, serve the bananas warm, and enjoy.

Mouth-Watering Salmon Egg Frittata

Recipe Makes 6 Servings.
Preparation Time: 40 minutes

Ingredients:

1 1/2 pounds salmon

2 tbsp. coconut oil

10 eggs

1 tbsp. chopped dill

1 tsp. chopped chives

1 tsp. salt

1 tsp. pepper

Directions:

First, preheat the air fryer to 375 degrees Fahrenheit. Next, add the coconut oil to a skillet on medium-high heat.

Allow the coconut oil to melt. Slice the salmon into small, bite-sized fillets. Salt and pepper the salmon on all sides and add them to the skillet. Allow them to cook for about four minutes.

Next, flip the salmon over to cook the other side. Cook this side for three minutes. Remove the salmon from the heat.

Next, grease a baking dish with coconut oil or another type of oil.

To the side, whisk the eggs, chives, dill, and additional salt and pepper.

Once the egg mixture is whisked, break up the salmon into even smaller pieces, and drop them into the baking dish. Pour the egg mixture over the salmon.

Next, place the egg pan in the air fryer. Cook for 25 minutes, or until the center of the frittata isn't wet any longer. It should be firm.

Remove the egg frittata and allow it to sit on the counter for ten minutes prior to slicing and serving.

Morning Pizza Quiche

Recipe Makes 4 Servings.
Preparation Time: 35 minutes

Ingredients:

8 eggs

1 tsp. coconut oil, melted

1/3 cup coconut milk

1/2 tsp. onion powder

1/2 tsp. garlic powder

1/2 tsp. salt

1 cup sliced mushrooms

1 cup sliced red peppers

3 ounces ground turkey

1/3 cup chopped green onions

2 tbsp. tomato paste

Directions:

First, preheat the air fryer to 375 degrees Fahrenheit.

Grease a baking dish with coconut oil or another oil of your choosing.

Next, crack the eggs into a medium-sized mixing bowl. Add salt, onion and garlic powder. Whisk the coconut milk in with the eggs. The mixture should begin to froth.

Next, add the vegetables and the ground turkey to the mixture. Stir until it's well-combined.

Next, pour this mixture into your greased pan. Add the tomato paste over the top.

Next, place this pizza quiche in the air fryer and allow it to cook for 25 minutes. The top should be crispy.

Allow the pizza quiche to rest for 10 minutes prior to serving, and enjoy.

Whole Food Air Fryer Chicken Recipes

Curry Coconut Chicken Meatballs

Recipe Makes 20 Meatballs.
Preparation Time: 35 minutes

Ingredients:

2 tbsp. cilantro, chopped

1/2 diced onion

1/2 cup chopped carrots

2 tbsp. chopped basil

1 tsp. ginger, ground

1/2 tsp. ground cumin

1/2 tsp. red chili flakes

Juice from one lime

1/2 tsp. salt

1/2 tsp. pepper

1 pound chicken, ground

1 tbsp. coconut aminos

Sauce Ingredients:

14 ounces coconut milk

1 tbsp. almond butter

1 tbsp. red curry paste

2 tsp. garlic, chopped

2 tbsp. lime juice

Directions:

First preheat the air fryer to 400 degrees Fahrenheit.

Next, place the cilantro, onion, carrots, basil, ginger, ground cumin, red chili flakes, juice from the lime, salt, pepper, and the coconut aminos in a food processor or a blender. Pulse the mixture until it's well blended.

Next, pour this mixture in with the chicken and stir well, using your hands so as not to overwork the meat.

Roll the chicken into 2-inch balls, and place them in a single line in your air fryer. You might have to do this in multiple batches.

Bake the chicken meatballs in the air fryer for 13 minutes, or until the chicken is cooked all the way through.

Afterwards, remove the meatballs from the air fryer and set them to the side, on a platter.

As the chicken meatballs cook, make the sauce in a separate skillet.

Do this by heating coconut milk over medium heat. Add the almond butter, red curry paste, garlic, and the lime juice. Simmer the mixture for 10 minutes. Stir continuously as it cooks.

Once the meatballs are cooked, add the meatballs to the sauce. Stir the meatballs in the sauce, heating for three minutes.

Serve the meatballs warm, and enjoy.

Yummy Tennessee's Best Fried Chicken

Recipe Makes 6 Servings.

Preparation Time: 10 minutes, after 30 minutes of marinating

Ingredients:

1 1/2 pounds chicken thighs

1 egg

1 tsp. garlic powder

3/4 cup almond flour

1/2 tsp. chili powder

1/2 tsp. paprika

Directions:

First, slice the chicken into fried chicken-like pieces, which are easier to eat. Coat the chicken with the spices—the garlic powder, chili powder, and paprika. Allow the chicken to sit with the spices for 30 minutes.

Preheat the air fryer to 400 degrees Fahrenheit at this time.

Next, add the egg to a medium-sized bowl, and whisk it using a fork.

To the side, add the almond flour to a separate bowl.

Next, dip each piece of chicken into the egg, and then coat the chicken pieces in the almond flour. Set the chicken in the air fryer basket as you prep them.

Next, fry the chicken in the air basket for about ten minutes, or until each of the chicken pieces is golden. Serve the chicken warm.

Indian Chicken

Recipe Makes 6 Servings.
Preparation Time: 45 minutes

Ingredients:

1 3/4 pounds chicken tenders, sliced in half

2 tbsp. minced garlic

1 tbsp. minced ginger

1 tsp. salt

1 tsp. paprika

1 tsp. cayenne pepper

2 tsp. turmeric

1/2 tsp. garam masala

1 tbsp. lemon juice

1 tbsp. olive oil

1/3 cup chopped cilantro

Directions:

First, stir together the spices—garlic, ginger, salt, paprika, cayenne pepper, turmeric, and the garam masala. Place the spices in a bowl, and then add the pieces of chicken, stirring well with your hands to coat the chicken fully. Let the chicken sit in the spices for 30 minutes to marinade.

Then, preheat the air fryer to 350 degrees Fahrenheit for five minutes. Afterwards, place the chicken in a single layer in the rack of the air fryer.

Brush half of the olive oil over the chicken on a single side. Then, cook the chicken in the air fryer for ten minutes.

Afterwards, flip the chicken, and brush them on the other side using the rest of the olive oil. Cook the chicken for five minutes more.

Next, remove the chicken and make sure the inside of the chicken has reached the temperature of 165 degrees Fahrenheit, to ensure that it's cooked all the way through.

Next, place the chicken on a side platter, and top it with lemon juice and cilantro.

Sunday Roast Rotisserie Chicken

Recipe Makes 6 Servings.
Preparation Time: 1 hour and 15 minutes

Ingredients:

1 rotisserie chicken, washed and patted dry

1 tsp. parsley, dried

1 tsp. garlic powder

1 tsp. black pepper

1 tsp. salt

2 tbsp. olive oil

Directions:

First, take the giblet from the inside of the chicken, wash the chicken, and then pat it dry.

Next, rub the olive oil over the chicken, coating it well. Season the chicken with the spices, rubbing them in well to coat.

Next, place the rotisserie chicken in the air fryer with the breast facing downward. Cook the chicken in the air fryer for 30 minutes at 350 degrees Fahrenheit.

Next, flip the chicken so that the belly faces up. Cook at 350 degrees Fahrenheit for 35 minutes this time.

Afterwards, check the inside of the chicken with your meat thermometer, making sure it reaches 165 degrees Fahrenheit.

Next, allow the chicken to rest for about 10 to 15 minutes before serving.

Lemony Chicken for Spring

Recipe Makes 1 Serving.
Preparation Time: 20 minutes

Ingredients:

1 chicken breast

Zest from one lemon

1/2 tsp. puree from garlic

1/2 tsp. garlic powder

1/2 tsp. onion powder

1/2 tsp. dried parsley

1/2 tsp. salt

1/2 tsp. pepper

Directions:

First, preheat the air fryer to 350 degrees Fahrenheit. To the side, add the seasonings and the lemon zest to a sheet of aluminum foil.

Season the chicken with salt and pepper, and then add the chicken to the aluminum foil sheet. Rub the chicken with the aluminum foil so that it's well-coated with seasonings.

Next, seal the chicken with the foil. Make sure that the chicken has nowhere to "breathe."

Next, flatten the aluminum foil with a rolling pin. Place the wrapped chicken in the air fryer basket for 15 minutes.

Afterwards, unwrap the chicken carefully, and serve warm.

Chicken Wings

Recipe Makes 4 Servings.
Preparation Time: 40 minutes

Ingredients:

2 pounds of chicken wings

1/2 tsp. cayenne pepper

1/2 tsp. paprika, smoked

1/2 tsp. garlic powder

1/2 tsp. cumin powder

Juice from 1/2 lemon

1/2 tsp. salt

Directions:

First, add the entire list of ingredients to a large bowl. Mix and toss the chicken wings so that they're well-coated.

Cover the chicken wings and allow them to marinate in the spices for 25 minutes.

Five minutes before cooking, preheat the air fryer to 360 degrees Fahrenheit.

Next, place the chicken wings in one layer in the air fryer's basket. You may have to do them in different batches.

Place the basket in the air fryer.

Cook the chicken wings in the air fryer for 15 minutes. Afterwards, serve the chicken wings warm, and enjoy.

Chicken Patties with a Crunchy Coconut Crust

Recipe Makes 6 Servings.
Preparation Time: 45 minutes

Ingredients:

1 pound ground chicken

1 egg

1/2 tsp. paprika

1 tsp. onion powder

1/2 tsp. salt

1/2 tsp. pepper

3/4 cup almond flour, separated

1/2 cup coconut oil, melted

1/2 cup coconut flakes, unsweetened

Directions:

First, preheat the air fryer to 375 degrees Fahrenheit.

In a medium-sized bowl, stir together the coconut flakes, 1/2 cup almond flour, and the salt and pepper.

To the side, in a separate bowl, stir together the rest of the almond flour, onion powder, paprika, extra salt and pepper, and the egg.

Next, melt the coconut oil in a skillet over medium heat. As it melts, make the chicken patties with your hands—taking about 2 tbsp. of the chicken and rolling it into a ball. Coat the chicken balls with the almond and coconut flake mixture.

Then, place the balls in the skillet, and flatten them, cooking on both sides for two minutes each.

Next, place the patties in the air fryer for five minutes. Serve the chicken patties warm, and enjoy.

Whole Food Air Fryer Beef Recipes

Spicy Whole Food Stuffed Peppers

Recipe Makes 2 Servings.
Preparation Time: 25 minutes

Ingredients:

5 green or red peppers

1/2 pound ground beef

1/2 tsp. cayenne pepper

1/2 tsp. ground pepper

1 cup spinach

1/2 tsp. chili powder

1 tbsp. pine nuts, crushed up

1 tsp. paprika

Directions:

First, preheat the air fryer to 415 degrees Fahrenheit.

Place the ground beef in a skillet over the stove. Cook until the beef is no longer pink, stirring occasionally.

While the beef cooks, slice the peppers in half and take out the insides. For one of the peppers, chop it into fine, bite-sized pieces.

When the beef is nearly finished, add the spinach to the skillet and allow it to wilt. Add the green pepper as well, along with the spices—the chili powder, cayenne, ground pepper, and the cumin.

After cooking this mixture for five minutes, stuff the green or red peppers with the ground beef mixture. Top each of the peppers with pine nuts.

Place the stuffed peppers in the air fryer and cook them for 17 minutes, or until the vegetables are very nearly soft.

Serve the stuffed peppers warm, and enjoy.

Whole Food Beef Meatballs

Recipe Makes 6 Servings.
Preparation Time: 15 minutes

Ingredients:

1 1/2 pounds ground beef

1 egg

3/4 cup almond flour

3 minced garlic cloves

2 tsp. onion powder

1 tsp. garlic powder

1/2 tsp. pepper

1 tsp. salt

1 tbsp. olive oil

Directions:

First, stir together the onion powder, almond flour, and the garlic powder in a medium-sized mixing bowl. Add the pepper and the salt and give the spice mixture a final good stir.

Add the garlic, egg, and the beef to the mixture, stirring it all together with your hands to ensure that you don't overwork the meat.

Next, make golf-ball-sized meatballs, rolling them in your hands. Place them on a platter to the side. As you do this, preheat your air fryer for five minutes to 400 degrees Fahrenheit.

Next, pour the olive oil into the bottom of the air fryer (just enough to coat), and add the meatballs. Make sure to leave space around the meatballs to ensure they don't touch each other or the sides of the air fryer. This might mean you need to do them in separate batches.

Next, cook the meatballs for 10 minutes. Afterwards, serve the meatballs warm and enjoy.

Beefy Nacho Pie

Recipe Makes 6 Servings.
Preparation Time: 40 minutes

Ingredients:

1 1/3 pound ground beef

1/2 tbsp. chili powder

1 tsp. cumin

1/2 tsp. garlic powder

1/2 tsp. cayenne pepper

1/4 tsp. coriander powder

1/4 tsp. garlic powder

1/2 cup water

Pie Crust Ingredients:

1 head of cauliflower, riced in a food processor

2 tbsp. coconut flour

1 egg

1/2 tsp. chili powder

1/2 tsp. salt

1/2 tsp. cumin

1/4 tsp. garlic powder

1 tbsp. chopped jalapeno peppers

Topping Ingredients:

1/2 sliced avocado

1 sliced tomato

Directions:

First, preheat the air fryer to 400 degrees Fahrenheit. Grease the inside of a casserole dish that can fit inside the air fryer (using olive oil or coconut oil).

Next, place the ground beef in a skillet and brown it over medium heat, stirring occasionally. When it's browned, remove it from the heat and drain a bit of the grease.

To the side, stir together the spices. When the spices are combined, add the water and stir well.

Next, pour this spice mixture into the beef skillet and stir well. Heat the skillet once more, over medium-high heat, and allow it to come to a boil. When it does begin to boil, turn the heat to LOW, and cover it, allowing it to simmer for five minutes.

While the ground beef cooks, process the cauliflower in a food processor until it looks like rice. Then, stir the cauliflower together with the rest of the pie crust ingredients: the coconut flour, egg, chili powder, salt, cumin, garlic powder, and chopped jalapenos.

Press the meat into the bottom of the casserole dish, so that it's flat. Then, press the pie crust over the top of the ground beef. Use a back of a spoon to make it flat.

Place the baking dish in the air fryer, and allow it to cook for 20 minutes. The pie crust edges should begin to brown. If the center isn't yet firm, allow it to cook a few minutes more.

Remove the pie from the air fryer, and allow it to cool for about five minutes prior to slicing. Add the avocado and the tomato, and serve warm.

Eggplant Lasagna

Recipe Makes 6 Servings.
Preparation Time: 15 minutes

Ingredients:

1 eggplant, medium-sized, sliced

1 1/2 pounds ground beef

2 cups tomato puree

1 large tomato, sliced

1 cup macadamia nuts

juice from 1/2 lemon

1/2 tsp. Italian herbs

1/2 tsp. salt

1 minced garlic clove

1/3 cup water

Directions:

First, add the macadamia nuts, lemon juice, Italian herbs, salt, garlic, and the water to a food processor. Process well until the mixture looks almost ricotta cheese-like. Taste the mixture and add salt and pepper if needed.

Next, add the ground beef to a skillet and allow it to brown for five minutes. Add the tomato puree. Salt and pepper the mixture, and stir well. Place the lid on the skillet and allow it to simmer on low heat throughout the rest of the process.

Next, slice the eggplant into flat disc-like forms. They should be about a half-inch thick. Sprinkle them with salt and pepper. Do the same with the tomato slices. Then, add the eggplant and tomato slices to the air fryer.

Cook the slices in the air fryer for 6 minutes on 350 degrees Fahrenheit.

Afterwards, assemble your lasagna "stacks." Do this by placing a slab of eggplant on the bottom of the air fryer, followed by meat, followed by eggplant, followed by tomato, and then a bit of the macadamia nut mixture. Once the stacks have been added to the air fryer, cook the lasagna stacks for four minutes more.

Afterwards, serve the eggplant lasagna stacks warm, and enjoy.

Whole Food Burgers

Recipe Makes 4 Servings.
Preparation Time: 20 minutes

Ingredients:

1 tsp. dried parsley

1 tsp. onion powder

1 tsp. oregano, dried

1/2 tsp. garlic powder

1 pound ground beef

1 tsp. sea salt

Directions:

First, preheat the air fryer to 350 degrees Fahrenheit for at least five minutes.

Next, stir together the seasonings in a medium-sized mixing bowl. Add the beef and use your hands to mix, making sure not to overwork.

Divide up the meat into four burger patties, placing a small indent with your thumb in the center of each patty to make sure they don't get too thick and pink in the middle.

Place the burger patties in the air fryer tray. Cook the burgers in the air fryer for 10 minutes to achieve "medium," or a bit longer if you want medium-well or well burgers.

Serve the burgers warm, and enjoy.

Whole Food Meatloaf

Recipe Makes 4 Servings.
Preparation Time: 25 minutes

Ingredients:

1 1/2 cups almond flour

1 egg

1 pound ground beef

2 tsp. salt

1/2 cup diced onion

1 tsp. dried basil

3 minced garlic cloves

1/2 cup tomato sauce

1/2 tsp. ground pepper

Directions:

First, preheat the air fryer to 350 degrees Fahrenheit.

Stir together the ground beef and the egg, along with the onion, almond flour, and the spices. Use your hands to stir. Then, add the tomato sauce and the garlic cloves, and continue to work the meat with your hands until you form a meatloaf-like form.

Place the meatloaf in the air fryer basket, and air fry the meatloaf for 24 minutes. Afterwards, remove the meatloaf carefully and allow it to rest on a side plate for 10 minutes before slicing and serving.

Vibrant Sweet Potato Pie with Beef

Recipe Makes 4 Servings.
Preparation Time: 1 hour

Ingredients:

1 pound ground beef

1 diced onion

3 minced garlic cloves

1 tbsp. coconut aminos

1/2 tsp. salt

1/2 tsp. nutmeg

1/2 tsp. Dijon mustard

1/2 tsp. black pepper

1/2 diced red pepper

2 cups chopped broccoli

2 cups chopped spinach

1 cup sliced mushrooms

2 sliced sweet potatoes, medium-size

2 tbsp. coconut oil

1 tsp. chopped parsley

1/4 cup chopped walnuts

Directions:

First, preheat the air fryer to 375 degrees Fahrenheit. Then, grease a pan that can fit in the air fryer with a bit of coconut oil.

Next, prep the sweet potatoes so that they're thin and "crust-like." Cover the bottom of the pan with these thin strips of sweet potatoes. The slices should kind of overlap so that none of the pan shows through.

Next, add the coconut oil to a skillet and allow it to melt over medium-high heat. Add the garlic and the onion. Cook for three minutes, and then add the mushrooms. Salt and pepper the mixture and cook for four minutes more.

At this time, add the nutmeg to the mixture, along with the ground beef. Give the mixture a good stir and then allow the ground beef to cook until it's brown.

At this time, add the Dijon mustard and the coconut aminos. Give the mixture a stir, and then add the spinach. Allow the spinach to wilt slightly before removing it from the heat and setting the skillet to the side.

Next, boil a pot of water. When the water begins to boil, place the broccoli florets inside, then immediately remove the pot from heat.

Next, drain the broccoli and place the broccoli florets over the top of the sweet potato pieces. Top the broccoli with the ground beef. Then, add the mushrooms and the peppers.

Then, add another layer of sweet potatoes in the same fashion as you did down below these layers.

Cover the pie with aluminum foil at this time. Place the pie in the air fryer, and cook for 45 minutes. Afterwards, remove the piece of aluminum foil, and bake for an additional 10 minutes. The potatoes should begin to brown at the edges.

Then, remove the pie from the air fryer, and allow it to cool for 10 minutes on a cooling rack. Then, garnish the pie with chopped walnuts and parsley. Serve the pie and enjoy.

Whole Food Air Fryer Pork Recipes

Flavor Explosion Peppery Pork Chops

Recipe Makes 6 Servings.
Preparation Time: 40 minutes

Ingredients:

1 egg white

1 cup almond flour

1 1/2 pound pork chops, sliced into easy-to-handle pieces

1 tbsp. olive oil

1 tsp. sea salt

1 tsp. ground black pepper

salt and pepper to taste

Directions:

First, pour the olive oil into the air fryer, to give the bottom a good glaze.

To the side, stir together salt, pepper, and the egg white, whisking well with a fork.

After slicing the pork chops, add them to the egg white and salt and pepper mixture, coating it well. Allow the pork to marinate for 25 minutes in the fridge.

At this time, add the pork chops to a large mixing bowl. Add the almond flour, and dredge the pork chops, making sure to coat them.

Shake out the pork chops and place them in the air fryer at this time. Cook the pork chops for 13 minutes at 355 degrees Fahrenheit. After every two minutes, make sure you shake the basket well.

After 13 minutes, adjust the temperature to 400 degrees Fahrenheit. Cook for six additional minutes. This will make the chops crispy. Shake every minute or so to prevent the chops from sticking to one another.

Serve the pork chops warm at this time, and enjoy.

Ginger Lime Pork Curry

Recipe Makes 6 Servings.
Preparation Time: 25 minutes

Ingredients:

1 1/2 pounds pork, cut into smaller pieces

1 tsp. coriander

1/2 tsp. chili powder

1 tsp. cumin

2 tsp. coconut oil

14 ounces coconut cream

1-inch sliced piece of ginger, chopped

Juice from a lime

Zest from a lime

3 minced garlic cloves

1/2 tsp. cinnamon

1/2 tsp. sea salt

1/2 tsp. pepper

1/2 diced onion

Directions:

First, add the pork to a mixing bowl. Add the spices to the bowl and stir well, making sure that the pork is coated. Allow it to marinate for about an hour (or overnight, if you have time).

Just before you're ready to cook, preheat the air fryer to 400 degrees Fahrenheit.

Add the coconut oil (melted in the microwave first), coconut cream, garlic, onion, and ginger to the pork mixture. Stir well. Pour this mixture into the air fryer baking dish at this time.

Next, cook the pork curry for 20 minutes, or until the curry is bubbling.

Remove the baking dish from the air fryer. Add the lime juice and the lime zest, along with extra salt. Give the mixture a stir and return it to the air fryer.

Cook the curry for five more minutes. Afterwards, serve the curry warm, and enjoy.

Chinese Pork Roast

Recipe Makes 4 Servings.
Preparation Time: 30 minutes

Ingredients:

6 tbsp. juice from orange

2 tbsp. coconut aminos

1 tbsp. apple cider vinegar

1 tsp. Chinese Five spice

3 tsp. garlic powder

1 pound pork belly

Directions:

First, slice the pork into thin slices. Pierce the slices using a fork.

Next, stir together the rest of the ingredients: orange juice, coconut aminos, apple cider vinegar, Chinese five spice, and the garlic powder.

Add the pork to a large bowl, and pour half of the spices mixture over the top. Coat the pork with the spices using your hands, making sure to reach every area of the meat. Allow the pork to marinate in the spices for 30 minutes.

Remove the pork from the bowl and place it in one layer in the air basket.

Next, heat the air fryer at 400 degrees Fahrenheit for 14 minutes. After seven minutes, flip the pork strips and baste them with some of the spice mixture.

As the pork cooks, place the rest of the spice mixture in the microwave and cook on HIGH for one minute. Stir the mixture every 15 seconds. This will allow the mixture to thicken.

When the meat has reached an internal temperature of 145 degrees Fahrenheit, remove the pork from the air fryer. Place the pork on a side platter and allow it to sit for 10 minutes.

Next, brush the pork with the sauce from the microwave, and serve warm.

Cinnamon Apple Pork Chops

Recipe Makes 4 Servings.
Preparation Time: 15 minutes

Ingredients:

4 bone-in pork chops

2 apples, sliced into 1/4-inch thick pieces

1 tsp. onion powder

1 tsp. cinnamon

1 tsp. sea salt

1 tsp. pepper

1 diced red pepper

3 tbsp. coconut oil

1 tbsp. sage, chopped roughly

2 tsp. chopped rosemary

Directions:

First, salt and pepper the pork chops on all sides. Add the cinnamon, rosemary, sage and the onion powder, and use your hands to rub it into the meat.

Heat the coconut oil in a skillet. Once it's melted, brown the pork chops on all sides for about two minutes each.

At this time, place the pork chops in the air fryer. Add the apples, red pepper and onions around the pork chops.

Cook the pork chops at 400 degrees Fahrenheit for eight minutes. Give the mixture a stir and then cook the pork for another six minutes.

Remove the pork from the air fryer and serve warm, with the apples and onions.

Spicy Chipotle Pork Chops

Recipe Makes 4 Servings.
Preparation Time: 15 minutes

Ingredients:

4 pork chops, one-inch thick, boneless

1/2 tsp. cumin

2 tbsp. coconut oil

1 tbsp. chili powder

2 minced garlic cloves

1/2 tsp. chipotle chili pepper spices

1 tsp. paprika

Sauce Ingredients:

1 cup coconut milk

1 tsp. liquid smoke

1/3 cup chopped cilantro

Garnish Ingredients:

Juice from a lime

1/2 cup chopped cilantro

Directions:

Preheat the air fryer to 400 degrees Fahrenheit.

Brush each of the pork chops with melted coconut oil. Then, rub the pork chops with the spices—the cumin, chili powder, garlic, chipotle chili pepper spice, and the paprika. Make sure to coat them well.

Next, place the pork chops in the air fryer. Cook for four minutes, then flip each pork chop to cook the other side.

While the pork chops cook in the air fryer, stir together the sauce ingredients—using a food processor to make very smooth. Cook the sauce on medium-low heat on the stove, reducing it slightly. Do this for three minutes.

Serve the pork chops warm, with the sauce poured over the top. Add a garnish of cilantro and lime juice.

Teriyaki Glaze Pork Chops

Recipe Makes 8 Servings.
Preparation Time: 25 minutes

Ingredients:

1/3 cup coconut aminos

1/2 tbsp. Dijon mustard

1-inch piece of grated ginger

3 minced garlic cloves

3 tbsp. coconut oil

1 tbsp. date paste

2 tbsp. balsamic vinegar

2 pounds pork tenderloins

Salt and pepper to taste

Directions:

First, preheat the air fryer to 400 degrees Fahrenheit.

Stir together the coconut aminos, Dijon mustard, ginger, garlic, date paste, balsamic vinegar, and a bit of salt and pepper for your sauce. Coat the pork tenderloins with the sauce, and add salt and pepper.

Next, heat a skillet on medium-high heat. Add the coconut oil to the skillet. Brown the pork tenderloins on all sides, for about two minutes each. Then, place the pork tenderloins in the air fryer.

Pour the remaining sauce over the pork tenderloins, and cook the tenderloins for 15 minutes in the preheated air fryer.

Afterwards, brush the pork tenderloins with any remaining sauce, and serve the pork warm.

Whole Food Air Fryer Fish Recipes

Salmon with Citrus Flare

Recipe Makes 4 Servings.
Preparation Time: 17 minutes

Ingredients:

4 salmon fillets

1/2 cup apple cider vinegar

2 tbsp. coconut oil

2 tbsp. minced garlic

Juicy from one lemon

½ tsp. pepper

½ tsp. salt

Directions:

First, preheat the air fryer at 400 degrees Fahrenheit. Season the salmon with salt and pepper.

After ten minutes of preheating, place the salmon fillets on the air fryer grill pan. Cook the salmon for six minutes.

While the salmon cooks, create the sauce to the side. Do this by sautéing the garlic in the coconut oil for three minutes. Afterwards, add the apple cider vinegar and the lemon juice. Bring the mixture to a boil.

The moment the mixture begins to boil, reduce the heat to its lowest setting. Cook the sauce for five minutes at this temperature.

Remove the sauce from the heat. When the salmon is finished, pour the sauce over the salmon, and serve warm.

Bay Area Shrimp Scampi

Recipe Makes 6 Servings.
Preparation Time: 20 minutes

Ingredients:

1 1/2 pounds shrimp (about 35 pieces, defrosted)

6 tbsp. coconut oil

3 minced garlic cloves

1 tsp. chives, dried

2 tsp. red pepper flakes

2 tbsp. lemon juice

1 tbsp. basil, fresh and chopped

1 tbsp. apple cider vinegar

Directions:

Preheat the air fryer to 330 degrees Fahrenheit.

Add the coconut oil, garlic, and the red pepper flakes to a pan. Allow the mixture to melt, stirring occasionally. Cook it for two minutes in the air fryer.

Next, add the lemon juice, chives, basil, apple cider vinegar, and the shrimp to the pan. Give the mixture a very slow, even stir.

Allow the shrimp to cook in the air fryer for five minutes. Stir about half-way through, but only once.

Afterwards, remove the pan from the air fryer. Allow the shrimp to rest on the counter for one minute, allowing the shrimp to cook in the hot coconut oil during this time.

Stir once more after a minute. Serve with basil over the top, and enjoy.

Pub's Best Air-Fried Cod (For Fish and Chips)

Recipe Makes 2 Servings.Preparation Time: 20 minutes

Ingredients:

2 fillets of cod

1 egg

1 tsp. salt

1 tbsp. almond milk

1/2 cup almond flour

1 tbsp. coconut oil

Directions:

First, preheat the air fryer to 370 degrees Fahrenheit.

To the side, whisk together the almond milk and the egg in a medium-sized bowl.

Next, pour the almond flour on a separate plate.

Pat the fillets of cod dry using a paper towel. Then, salt it well, covering all sides with a bit of salt.

Dip the cod fillets into the egg, and then immediately dredge the fillets in the almond flour. Make sure that you fully coat the fillets.

Place the cod in the air fryer basket. Drizzle the cod pieces with melted coconut oil (can be melted either in the microwave or on the stovetop).

Next, cook the fillets in the air fryer for 10 minutes, shaking all the time.

After the cod has finished, remove them from the air basket and serve warm with some of the whole food fries listed in the "snack" chapter.

Crispy Prawns

Recipe Makes 4 Serving.
Preparation Time: 19 minutes

Ingredients:

30 king prawns

2 tbsp. coriander

2 tbsp. minced garlic

1 cauliflower head

Juice from one lemon

1 tsp. garlic powder

1 tsp. onion powder

1 tsp. red curry paste

1 tsp. Chinese 5 spice

2 eggs

1 tsp. salt

1 tsp. pepper

Directions:

First, clean your prawns and add them to a medium-sized mixing bowl.

Either in your microwave or your stovetop, melt the coconut oil. Toss the garlic and the prawns in the melted coconut oil for two minutes. Then, add the prawns back to the mixing bowl.

Next, add the lemon juice, red curry paste, salt, and pepper to the bowl. Stir well. Then, place aluminum foil or cling wrap over the bowl, and allow the prawns to marinate for one hour in the refrigerator.

While the prawns are prepping in the fridge, make the crumble for the outside of the prawns. Do this by adding the cauliflower to a food processor, crumbling it until it becomes like a "meal."

Add the garlic powder, onion powder, and the Chinese 5 spice to the food processor and blend until it's all well-mixed. Afterwards, pour the mixture into a separate mixing bowl.

In a separate bowl, whisk the eggs.

Next, remove the prawns from the mixing bowl in the fridge, and pat them dry with a towel or a paper towel. Toss the prawns in the cauliflower crumble mixture. Then, add them to the egg, then add them back to the breadcrumb-like mixture.

Place the prawns on a baking sheet, and cook them in the air fryer at 375 degrees Fahrenheit for 10 minutes.

Afterwards, serve the prawns with fresh lemon, and enjoy.

Cajun Spicy Salmon

Recipe Makes 1 Servings.
Preparation Time: 10 minutes

Ingredients:

1 salmon fillet

1 tsp. Cajun seasoning

Juice from 1/2 lemon, to serve

Directions:

First, preheat the air fryer to 375 degrees Fahrenheit for at least five minutes.

After washing the salmon, pat it dry. Sprinkle the salmon with the Cajun seasoning, making sure you coat all sides of it.

Then, add the salmon to the air fryer. Air fry the salmon for seven minutes with the skin side up.

Afterwards, serve the salmon immediately, adding lemon juice for flavor.

Whole Food Air Fryer Vegetarian Recipes

No Chickpea Falafels

Recipe Makes 16 Falafels.
Preparation Time: 40 minutes

Ingredients:

2 cups cauliflower, minced in a food processor

3/4 cup chopped onion

1/2 cup almond flour

1/3 cup chopped parsley leaves

1/3 cup chopped cilantro leaves

1 egg

1 tbsp. arrowroot flour

1 tsp. salt

3 tsp. cumin

1 tsp. pepper

1/2 tsp. turmeric

3 tbsp. olive oil

1/2 tsp. chili powder

Dressing Ingredients:

1/2 cup sesame oil

1/3 cup tahini

2 tsp. date paste

2 tbsp. lemon juice

1/2 tsp. lemon zest

Directions:

First, preheat the air fryer to 400 degrees Fahrenheit.

Next, blend together the chopped onion, almond flour, parsley, cilantro, egg, arrowroot flour, salt, cumin, pepper, turmeric, and chili powder—that is, everything except the cauliflower and the olive oil. Blend the ingredients in a food processor until it's well mixed and minced.

Afterwards, add the cauliflower to the food processor and pulse until the mixture is well combined.

Next, using your hands, form the mixture into falafel balls. Brush the balls with olive oil, and place them in the air fryer basket.

Cook the falafel balls for 15 minutes in the air fryer basket, shaking every few minutes to ensure they don't stick together.

While the falafel balls cook, bring the dressing ingredients into a food processor or blender and blend until smooth.

Serve the falafel balls warm or cold, with a drizzle of the dressing.

Whole Food Ratatouille

Recipe Makes 4 Servings.
Preparation Time: 30 minutes

Ingredients:

3 tbsp. olive oil

3 smashed garlic cloves

2 sprigs of oregano

2 sliced squashes, summer

2 sliced red peppers

1 sliced eggplant

3 tbsp. chopped thyme leaves

1 cup tomato puree

2 sliced zucchinis

1 sliced red onion

3 sliced tomatoes

1 tsp. salt

1 tsp. pepper

Directions:

First, preheat the air fryer to 375 degrees Fahrenheit.

Next, heat the olive oil and the garlic in a skillet over medium-low heat. Cook the garlic for one minute. Then, remove the skillet from the stove and add the oregano. Allow the oregano to sit in the olive oil for 15 minutes.

Afterwards, toss out the garlic and the oregano, and drizzle the olive oil into the bottom of a baking dish that can fit inside your air fryer.

Next, spread the tomato puree into the baking dish, over the olive oil. Add the eggplant, onion, zucchini, summer squash, pepper, zucchini, and the tomato in whatever layers you choose. Make sure the vegetables are packed tightly.

Brush a bit of extra tomato puree over the top, and drizzle a bit of extra oil over the vegetables. Add salt and pepper to the top.

Place the baking dish in the air fryer, and bake in the air fryer for 30 minutes. Allow the ratatouille to cool for 10 minutes prior to serving.

Delightful Veggie Quiche

Recipe Makes 4 Servings.
Preparation Time: 40 minutes

Ingredients:

1 1/2 heads of broccoli, chopped

1 diced onion

1 diced tomato

4 diced carrots

1 tsp. dried thyme

1 tsp. dried parsley

3 eggs

1/2 cup almond milk

1/2 tsp. salt

1/2 tsp. pepper

Directions:

Chop the vegetables: broccoli, onion, and the carrots. Add them to the air fryer and cook at 300 degrees Fahrenheit for 12 minutes. The vegetables should be soft.

Next, to the side, stir together the seasonings in a medium-sized bowl. Add the almond milk and the eggs, and stir well.

After the vegetables are finished cooking, add them to the bottom of a quiche dish or pan. Add the tomatoes over the top, spreading them out. Pour the egg mixture over the top of the vegetables.

Place the quiche dish in the air fryer. Cook the quiche for 20 minutes at 370 degrees Fahrenheit. Allow the quiche to cool prior to slicing and serving.

Vegetable Spaghetti Squash

Recipe Makes 3 Servings.
Preparation Time: 55 minutes

Ingredients:

1/2 spaghetti squash

1 tbsp. grape seed oil

1/2 tsp. salt

1/2 tsp. pepper

1 chopped Poblano pepper

5 grape tomatoes

Directions:

Prep the spaghetti squash, first, by slicing off the ends of the spaghetti squash and slicing it in half. Clean out the seeds.

Then, slice the grape tomatoes and the Poblano pepper. Salt and pepper the inside of the spaghetti squash, and then add the grape seed oil, drizzling it over the extent of the squash.

Next, preheat the air fryer to 350 degrees Fahrenheit.

Place the squash in the air fryer, and cook for 30 minutes. Next, add the tomatoes and the poblano pepper to the air fryer. Add a bit more salt and pepper.

Cook the pepper for another 15 minutes.

Next, remove the squash from the air fryer, and shred up the squash with the vegetables, until it's well-mixed. Serve warm, and enjoy.

Whole Food Air Fryer Side Dish Recipes

Curry Cauliflower

Recipe Makes 4 Servings.
Preparation Time: 20 minutes.

Ingredients:

2 pounds chopped cauliflower

1 tbsp. olive oil

2 tsp. curry powder

Juice from 1/2 lemon

1 tsp. salt

1 tsp. pepper

2 tbsp. chopped basil

Directions:

First, preheat the air fryer to 400 degrees Fahrenheit.

After slicing up the cauliflower, add them to a large bowl. Stir the cauliflower with the olive oil, coating it well. Next, add the curry powder and toss the cauliflower well so that it's coated in the spice.

Add salt and pepper and toss once more.

Spread the cauliflower in the air fryer. Cook for 15 minutes. The cauliflower should become a golden brown.

Afterwards, return the cauliflower florets to the mixing bowl. Add the lemon juice and toss well. Serve with the basil and any additional salt and pepper, and enjoy.

Air Fried Brussels Sprouts

Recipe Makes 2 Servings.
Preparation Time: 10 minutes

Ingredients:

2 cups Brussels sprouts, sliced in half

1 tbsp. balsamic vinegar

1 tbsp. olive oil

½ tsp. salt

Directions:

First, toss the Brussels sprouts with the olive oil, vinegar, and the salt.

Add the Brussels sprouts to the air fryer basket, and add it to the air fryer. Cook the sprouts for 10 minutes at 400 degrees Fahrenheit.

Throughout the cooking process, shake the sprouts in the air fryer basket every two minutes or so. The sprouts should be crispy.

Serve warm, and enjoy.

Savory Cauliflower Tortillas

Recipe Makes 6 Tortillas.
Preparation Time: 40 minutes

Ingredients:

1 head of cauliflower

1/3 cup chopped cilantro

2 eggs

Juice from ½ lime

1 tsp. salt

1 tsp. pepper

Directions:

First, preheat the air fryer to 375 degrees Fahrenheit.

Trim the cauliflower head, and slice it into florets. Pulse the cauliflower in a food processor to create a kind of smooth consistency.

Next, place the cauliflower in a medium-sized bowl. Microwave it for two minutes on medium-high heat. Afterwards, stir, and microwave for an additional minute. Then, squeeze out the liquid, or as much as you can, using a towel or a paper towel.

To the side, whisk the eggs. Add the cilantro, lime, cauliflower, and the salt and pepper. Stir well. Shape the mixture into tortilla-like pieces.

Place the tortillas in the air fryer, flat. You will have to do these in separate batches. Cook the tortillas for eight minutes. Then, flip the tortillas and cook for an additional seven minutes. The tortillas should be set. Remove them from the air fryer and allow them to cool.

Optional: Just before serving, brown the tortillas in a skillet on medium-high, for one or two minutes on each side. Then, serve and enjoy.

Air Fryer Asparagus

Recipe Makes 4 Servings.
Preparation Time: 15 minutes

Ingredients:

1/2 bunch of asparagus, trimmed at the bottom

2 tsp. olive oil

1 tsp. sea salt

1 tsp. pepper

Directions:

First, trim the two inches from the bottom of the asparagus, and place the asparagus in the air fryer basket. Drizzle a bit of olive oil over the spears, and then add salt and pepper.

Next, bake the asparagus in the air fryer at 400 degrees Fahrenheit for 10 minutes. Afterwards, serve the asparagus immediately.

Paleo-Friendly Butternut Squash Soufflé

Recipe Makes 6 Servings.
Preparation Time: 1 hour

Ingredients:

1 butternut squash, medium-sized

1/2 cup coconut milk

4 eggs, separated yolks from whites

1 tsp. salt

1 tsp. pepper

Directions:

First, preheat the air fryer to 350 degrees Fahrenheit.

Grease a soufflé dish (that can fit in the air fryer) with a bit of coconut oil or other whole-food-friendly oil.

Next, poke the squash with your fork, all over the place. Place the squash in the air fryer for 15 minutes, or until it's tender.

After the squash cools for a bit, slice it in half and remove the seeds. Add the flesh of the squash into a food processor or a blender, making sure to be careful not to burn yourself.

Next, add the egg yolks, salt, pepper, and the coconut milk to the food processor or blender and blend well until smooth. Pour this mixture into a large mixing bowl at this time.

To the side, use a fork to whip the egg whites until they create stiff peaks. Fold the egg whites into the rest of the squash mixture.

Pour the mixture into the soufflé dish at this time. Then, add the dish to the air fryer, and bake for 40 minutes.

Remove the dish carefully and allow the squash to cool for five to ten minutes prior to serving.

Whole Food Air Fryer Snack Recipes

Avocado Fries

Recipe Makes 8 Servings.
Preparation Time: 25 minutes

Ingredients:

2 avocados

1 egg

1 tsp. salt

1 tsp. garlic powder

1 tsp. onion powder

3/4 cup almond flour

Directions:

First, prep the avocado into slices (tossing out the pit and peel). Next, crack the egg in a small bowl. Whisk the egg using a fork.

In a separate bowl, stir together the salt, garlic powder, onion powder, and the almond flour. Dredge the avocado in the egg, and then dredge each slice in the almond flour mixture.

Add the avocado fries to the air fryer basket, making sure they don't touch one another or overlap.

Air fry the avocado fries for 12 minutes at 400 degrees Fahrenheit. After six minutes, shake the air fryer basket to flip the fries over.

Serve the avocado fries warm, and enjoy.

Crispy Zucchini Fries

Recipe Makes 6 Servings.
Preparation Time: 15 minutes

Ingredients:

3 large zucchinis
1 tsp. garlic powder
1/2 tsp. onion powder
1 cup almond flour
1 egg
1/2 tsp. salt
1/2 tsp. pepper

Directions:

First, preheat the air fryer to 400 degrees Fahrenheit.

Slice the zucchini in half, long-ways. Do this four times for each zucchini to produce long fries. Then, slice those in half once more. Do it until you reach your desired "thickness" for zucchini fries.

Next, crack the egg into a small-sized bowl. Whisk well. In a separate bowl, stir together the almond flour, garlic powder, onion powder, and the salt and pepper.

Dredge the zucchini fries in the egg, and then dredge them in the almond flour mixture. Add them to the air fryer once they're well-coated.

Cook the zucchini fries in the air fryer for 10 minutes. They should become golden brown. Serve the fries warm.

Spicy Kale Chips

Recipe Makes 6 Servings.
Preparation Time: 12 minutes

Ingredients:

6 cups kale, de-stemmed and torn into smaller pieces

2 tbsp. olive oil

2 tsp. onion powder

1 tsp. garlic powder

1 tsp. chili powder

1/2 tsp. salt

1/2 tsp. pepper

Directions:

After prepping the kale, toss it in the spices and the olive oil until it's well-coated. Then, add the kale to the basket of the air fryer.

Cook the kale chips in the air fryer at 380 degrees Fahrenheit for five minutes. Shake the basket every minute or so.

Serve the kale chips crispy and enjoy.

"Tater Tots" Minus the Potatoes

Recipe Makes 24 Tots.
Preparation Time: 45 minutes

Ingredients:

1/2 medium-sized spaghetti squash
1 sliced scallion
1/2 tbsp. olive oil
1/2 tsp. salt
1/2 tsp. pepper

Directions:

First, preheat the air fryer to 350 degrees Fahrenheit.

Next, prep the spaghetti squash. Do this by slicing the ends off, and then slicing the entire squash in half. You'll only need one half for this recipe (although you can of course double it for double the tots).

Next, salt and pepper the squash. Add the olive oil. Place the squash in the air fryer, and cook for 20 minutes.

Afterwards, remove the squash from the air fryer. Using a fork, remove the strands of spaghetti squash, and toss out the skin.

Place the squash strands on a kitchen towel, and roll them up. Wring out the moisture. Then, place the strands in a bowl. Slice up the strands an additional time, using a large knife.

Next, add more salt and pepper, along with the scallions.

Then, stir the mixture well, adding additional olive oil if it isn't moist enough. At this time, press the mixture into a muffin tin, and press them down using your fingers.

Afterwards, place the muffin tin into the air fryer, and fry the tots for 10 minutes. At this time, remove the tins from the air fryer, and flip them over. Cook for an additional 10 minutes. The tots should be golden brown.

Afterwards, serve the tots warm, and enjoy.

Spiralized Sweet Potato Fries

Recipe Makes 2 Servings.
Preparation Time: 12 minutes

Ingredients:

1 sweet potato

1/2 tbsp. olive oil

1 tsp. salt

need a spiralizer for preparation

Directions:

First, spiralize the sweet potato into long, thin spirals. Toss the sweet potato with olive oil and salt. Add the sweet potato spirals to your air fryer.

Cook the fries in the air fryer at 400 degrees Fahrenheit for ten minutes. Shake the air fryer basket frequently, tossing the fries around to allow them to grow crispy—but never stick together.

Serve the fries warm, and enjoy.

Spicy Cauliflower Morsels

Recipe Makes 6 Servings.
Preparation Time: 25 minutes

Ingredients:

1 cauliflower heat, sliced into florets

2 tsp. garlic powder

1 tbsp. olive oil

1/2 tsp. pepper

1/2 tsp. salt

1 tbsp. coconut oil

1/2 cup Frank's hot sauce (it is whole food approved)

Directions:

First, preheat the air fryer to 450 degrees Fahrenheit. Next, place the cauliflower in a plastic bag. Add the olive oil, and shake the cauliflower to coat it.

Add the garlic powder, salt, and the pepper. Close the bag and shake it well. The cauliflower should be coated in spices.

Next, add the cauliflower to the air fryer. Cook the florets for ten minutes, shaking the air fryer basket every two minutes to ensure they get crispy—but don't stick together.

Remove the florets from the air fryer. To the side, melt the coconut oil in a glass bowl in the microwave, or on the stovetop. Once it's melted, add the hot sauce. Stir well.

Toss the cauliflower in the hot sauce mixture, coating it well.

Place the cauliflower back in the air fryer. Cook for five more minutes, shaking in the air fryer every minute or so. Serve warm, and enjoy.

Roasted Almonds with Garlic

Recipe Makes 8 Servings.
Preparation Time: 11 minutes

Ingredients:

2 cups almonds

1 tbsp. garlic powder

1 tsp. paprika

1/2 tsp. ground black pepper

1 tbsp. coconut aminos

Directions:

First, stir together the coconut aminos, garlic powder, paprika, and the pepper in a medium-sized bowl. You should have a paste. Add the almonds at this time, and stir well, coating them.

Add the almonds to the air fryer basket. Cook in the air fryer for eight minutes at 320 degrees Fahrenheit. Make sure you shake the basket every two minutes to prevent sticking.

Allow them to cool for about fifteen minutes. Then, serve, or store for later.

CPSIA information can be obtained
at www.ICGtesting.com
Printed in the USA
LVHW101237300121
677866LV00009B/75

9 781913 982331